DEMYSTIFYING CONTENT DESIGN

BY

Azza Elarabi

For my brother, Dr. Yassir Al-Arabi, who has continuously encouraged and supported me throughout my professional and personal journey.

Special thanks to Rahel Anne Bailie for her invaluable input and support

© 2023 Azza Elarabi. All rights reserved.

TABLE OF CONTENTS

1. Who this book is for 4
2. What exactly is content design? 5
3. The difference between content design and UX writing 8
4. The relationship between content design and content strategy 9
5. The different roles content designers work with 11
6. How much do content designers earn? 13
7. The challenges of being a content designer 15
8. Is a career in content design right for you? 17
9. What companies look for when hiring content designers 19
10. Examples of content design job postings 21
11. Your first steps towards a career in content design 29
12. Get started with an introductory content design course 31
Resources 32
About the author 33

1. WHO THIS BOOK IS FOR

I wrote this compact book to shed light on the rapidly growing strategic field of content design. After reading this book, you will have a solid understanding of what content design is, how it differs from user experience (UX) writing and how content design sits within the broader field of content strategy. You'll know which skills to develop as an aspiring content designer and what companies look for when hiring content designers.

Read this book if:

- You are considering pursuing a career as a content designer.

- You work with content designers and would like to understand better what they do.

- You are a business leader or entrepreneur considering investing in content as a strategic business asset.

2. WHAT EXACTLY IS CONTENT DESIGN?

The history of content design goes back to the 1950s, when the Society of Technical Communication (STC) was formed to advance the field of technical communication.

With the growth of online content in the early 2000s, STC played a pivotal role in supporting technical writers, who produced work now carried out by content designers and writing technical documentation.

The term 'content design' was more recently coined by Sarah Winters when she led an effort at the UK government's Government Digital Service to consolidate over 400 government websites into a single site that served its users.

Content design is a growing specialization in user experience grounded in solving user problems with content that addresses their needs in the format they expect it and when they need it. When a user is looking for information or needs to do a task, the content design ensures the content is relevant and conveyed in the most appropriate and timely format and through the right channels.

In her book 'Content Design,' Winters describes the discipline as a 'way of thinking.'

I couldn't agree more. Content design is about solving user problems with content–regardless of the content's format.

In my experience, the closest concept to content design is product design. There's more overlap between what product designers and content designers do.

Demystifying Content Design

As product designers follow a design process, content design has a process, and it typically includes:

1. Conducting research

This step involves gathering and analyzing the data and insights that inform the content strategy and design. Content designers may use various research methods, such as user interviews, surveys, analytics, competitor analysis, and content audits, to identify the user's goals, pain points, and preferences.

2. Planning

This step involves defining the content's scope, structure, and messaging that align with the user's journey and the business objectives. Content designers may use various planning tools, such as user flows, personas, information architecture, and content models, to organize and visualize the content design.

3. Content creation

This step involves writing, editing, and designing the content that meets the user's needs and supports the business objectives. Content designers may use various creation tools, such as style guides, tone of voice, typography, and visual design, to ensure the content's consistency and coherence.

4. Testing

This step involves evaluating the content's usability, accessibility, and effectiveness by involving the users in the testing process. Content designers may use various testing methods, such as usability testing, A/B testing, or user feedback, to gather and analyze the data and insights that inform the content improvements.

5. Iteration

Based on the testing phase results, the content may be optimized to improve its effectiveness and usability. This may involve making changes to the content itself and changes to the overall product design.

Content design is changing how companies think about content's role in digital products. Content used to be an afterthought, often 'added' to a product towards the end of the design process.

But as more companies adopt a 'content-first way of thinking,' content is quickly becoming pivotal to how we create useful, relevant and delightful user experiences.

3. THE DIFFERENCE BETWEEN CONTENT DESIGN AND UX WRITING

You've probably come across content design and UX writing being used interchangeably. That's because the two fields are closely related. Both aim to solve user and business problems by understanding users' needs and mapping content requirements to customer journeys.

The primary difference is that **while UX writing focuses on UI copy, content design is a broader field that considers all forms of content** as solutions, depending on the user problem. Content design solutions may include videos, calculator tools, maps, forms, calendar tools, and many other formats.

UX writing typically involves the creation of microcopy or small pieces of text strategically placed throughout the user interface to guide the user through a product.

Content designers also craft UX copy to improve digital product usability–it's just one of many types of content they use.

It's fair to say that UX writing is part of content design. As I explain in the next chapter, content design is part of the broader content strategy discipline.

Carrie Hane, Co-author of 'Designing Connected Content,' sums up the link between UX writing, content design and content strategy eloquently:

Not sure which post to reply to the thread... I think UX writing is part of content design. Perhaps even one part of the execution of the content design, which is in itself a part of content strategy.

4. THE RELATIONSHIP BETWEEN CONTENT DESIGN AND CONTENT STRATEGY

If you're familiar with content strategy, you might wonder how it relates to content design. Think of content strategy as an umbrella discipline. **Content strategists are concerned with everything related to the content lifecycle to ensure the right content is served to the right audience at the right stage of the customer journey, through the right channels and in the right format**. Phew, that's a lot! And this is why we consider content strategy to be a **broad discipline that involves the planning for creation, dissemination and governance of content**.

Content design falls under this umbrella. Without user-driven, logically structured content that aids users in completing tasks, content cannot do its job, and the user experience fails. However, content design's scope does not necessarily encompass people, content governance, or content operations, while content strategy's scope does.

Also, as part of their work on digital products, content designers usually collaborate with other areas of the business that create content, such as customer experience and marketing. But, content designers aren't typically responsible for these other content types, while content strategists may be responsible for them depending on the scope of their content strategy and the business and user problem they're looking to solve.

So while there is an overlap between content design and content strategy, the two disciplines usually have different scopes. Content strategy is the umbrella and content design is more focused on content's usability and the user experience.

Remember, the ultimate goal of content strategy and content design is to create value for customers and the business, although in different ways. Due to this overlap, studying content strategy can make you a better content designer and is a direction to consider.

You'll learn new methodologies and tools to assess and improve content with the user and business in mind. You'll also learn to assess the entire ecosystem and be better able to connect the dots between UX content and other content types that ultimately affect customers' overall experience and their perception of a brand. These are a few examples of how studying content strategy has helped me, but there are a lot more examples!

If you're considering a career in content design, I advise you to gain some training in content strategy approaches and methodologies. You don't need to pursue a two-year master's degree as I did but expand your knowledge, and you will ultimately become a stronger content designer.

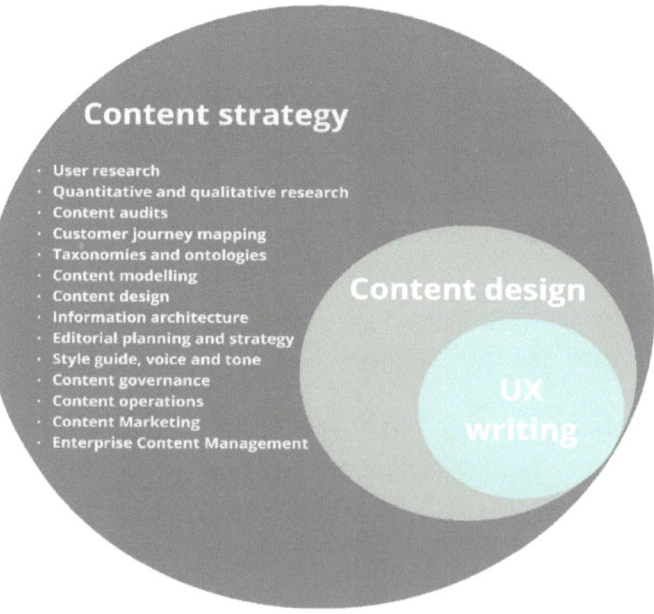

5. THE DIFFERENT ROLES CONTENT DESIGNERS WORK WITH

Content designers work closely with various other disciplines and roles to create effective content and user experiences. If you're considering a career in content design, you'll need to be familiar with the key roles and disciplines that you'll collaborate with:

User Experience (UX) designers:

Content designers work closely with UX designers to make sure the content they create aligns with the overall user experience strategy and design. They collaborate on the design process from user research to ideation, content strategy, and validation.

Writers and editors:

Often, content designers are responsible for crafting copy but may also work closely with other writers and editors to create effective, engaging, and accurate content. As a content designer, you'll collaborate on content ideation, writing and editing, and content formatting.

Software developers and engineers:

Content designers work with developers to ensure that the content they create is technically feasible and can be implemented on digital platforms. This includes defining content formats and creating copy strings that are scalable and ready to implement.

Product managers:

Content designers work closely with product managers to understand the user needs and goals for the product, and to align the content strategy with the product vision and roadmap. They collaborate on content planning, content testing, and content optimization for product features.

Customer support teams:

Content designers work with customer support teams to help create effective support documentation and help content. Consistency and alignment between product content and the wider content ecosystem is crucial because it impacts the overall customer experience. This means collaborating with customer support teams to ensure accurate and consistent information is conveyed through support articles, user manuals, and other support materials.

Marketing teams:

Depending on their scope, content designers may work with marketing teams to create effective marketing campaigns that align with the brand voice and tone. They collaborate on tasks such as campaign ideation, content creation, and campaign optimization for various marketing channels.

6. HOW MUCH DO CONTENT DESIGNERS EARN?

Content design is an exciting field that lets you flex your problem-solving muscles to create value for people. That's very rewarding. There's also the remuneration and rewards that come with the role—especially if you work in the tech industry. There's no easy answer to the question of how much content designers make because this depends on many factors, including seniority, location, the hiring company and which sector it belongs to, and many more.

According to a 2022 survey conducted by UX Writing Hub, the global average salary for writers in tech was $67,000.

Remember that salary ranges vary depending on geographic location, even within the United States. And overall, tech salaries are higher in the United States than in other regions such as Europe and Asia.

Here is an outline of the top 10 countries by median UX writing salaries, according to the survey:

Country	Median annual salary for writers in tech 2022
United States	$115,000
Australia	$107,079
Switzerland	$102,640
Hong Kong	$80,343
Norway	$80,039
Israel	$78,614
Ireland	$78,524
Netherlands	$76,342
Singapore	$73,828
Canada	$71,718

Source: UX Writing Hub

As you can see, salaries vary from country to country and city to city. This makes sense as demand for the role and cost of living also varies greatly.

7. THE CHALLENGES OF BEING A CONTENT DESIGNER

We've talked about the rewards you can look forward to as a content designer. But the role isn't without its challenges. Here are some:

Balancing creativity with strategy:

Content designers need to be creative in their approach to content creation while also adhering to the overall content strategy and design principles. Balancing creativity with strategy can be challenging, as it requires a deep understanding of the brand voice and tone, as well as the user needs and goals.

Meeting deadlines:

Content designers often work on multiple projects simultaneously, each with its deadlines and priorities. Meeting these deadlines can be challenging, especially when there are competing demands for their time and attention.

Keeping up with changing technology:

Content design is a rapidly evolving field, and new technologies and platforms emerge often. Staying up-to-date with the latest trends and technologies can be challenging and requires a commitment to ongoing learning and professional development.

Collaboration with cross-functional teams:

Content designers need to work closely with other disciplines and roles to create effective content and user experiences. Collaboration can be challenging when there are differing opinions or conflicting priorities among team members.

Content design is often misunderstood and confused with copywriting. You may need to constantly educate other roles to get a seat at the table and be involved throughout the product design and development process.

Dealing with feedback and criticism:

Content designers need to be open to feedback and criticism on their work and use this feedback to iterate and improve their designs. As I like to put it, everyone can "write," so your colleagues are likely to give you feedback on what you've created, even if said feedback is not based on craft principles and best practices. Dealing with negative feedback or criticism can be challenging, especially when it is not constructive or helpful. You'll need to be patient and believe in your skills and expertise.

Managing expectations:

Content designers need to manage stakeholder expectations effectively and ensure that their designs meet the needs and goals of all stakeholders. This can be challenging when there are conflicting priorities or limited resources available.

Balancing multiple priorities:

Because content designers often work across multiple teams, you'll need to balance demands competing for your time and attention.

8. IS A CAREER IN CONTENT DESIGN RIGHT FOR YOU?

I believe you can become a content designer with the right skills and passion.

Naturally, you'll have to have the right motivation.

If you're looking to jump on the bandwagon of getting into the user experience field for a high-paying job, you might not be in it for the right reasons.

But if you're more excited about solving complex user and business problems with content, then content design could prove a rewarding career.

Why specifically content, though? Why not product design or user research? After all, you'd also solve user and business problems through these disciplines.

It all depends on what you want and whether you have the right skills for your chosen path.

For me, content design is interesting for a number of reasons. First, content is how we communicate with customers. Without content, a digital product is a user interface that does nothing– despite how beautiful it looks.

As content strategy experts and pioneers Rahel Anne Bailie and Noz Urbina explain in their book 'Content Strategy: Connecting the dots between business, brand, and benefits,' users usually visit a digital product for three reasons: 1) to be informed of something, 2) to complete a task or transaction and 3) to engage with a brand.

Content is the core of any digital product; let no one tell you otherwise!

Second, content design enables me to empathize with users' needs through communication.

Now imagine the opportunity to make a product usable and delightful for users through the content you design. Plus, the business impact you would deliver through your strategic problem-solving and craft. These are the aspects of my job that I love most, and they're what motivate me every day.

If you believe in the power of content, and what I've described resonates, then content design could be right for you.

Not so fast, though! Motivation and passion for the field are undoubtedly crucial but not enough. You need to have the right skill set for the job. Read on to find out what you'll need to demonstrate to be considered for content design roles.

9. WHAT COMPANIES LOOK FOR WHEN HIRING CONTENT DESIGNERS

To make the cut as a content designer, you'll need to have a combination of technical skills and behavioral competencies or 'soft skills.' Here are some of the key factors that companies consider when hiring content designers:

Strong writing skills:

If you're designing content, you must understand what makes good content and be able to create it. You'll need to demonstrate that you can craft clear, useful and engaging content that helps users complete tasks.

Understanding of user experience:

A strong understanding of user UX design is essential for content designers, as they need to create content that is easy to navigate and enhances the overall user experience.

Creative problem-solving skills:

Content designers must develop creative solutions to content challenges and adapt quickly to changing requirements and priorities.

Technical proficiency:

Companies look for candidates proficient in relevant content design methodologies such as customer journey mapping, content modeling, information architecture and UX writing. You'll also be expected to be familiar with design tools like Figma.

Attention to detail:

Content designers need to have a keen eye for detail and be able to spot errors and inconsistencies in text, design, and formatting.

Collaboration skills:

Content designers often work as part of a team, so companies look for candidates able to collaborate effectively with other designers, writers, and stakeholders.

Understanding of brand voice and tone:

Companies look for candidates with a good understanding of their brand's voice and tone who can create content consistent with the brand's messaging and values.

Strong portfolio:

A strong portfolio that showcases a range of design and content creation skills is essential for content designers. Companies look for candidates who have created effective, engaging content for various digital platforms and audiences. When presenting your portfolio, you'll need to explain the problems you solved, the data that guided your decisions, the solutions you crafted, and your results.

10. EXAMPLES OF CONTENT DESIGN JOB POSTINGS

Before you apply for content design jobs, it's important to research the job requirements and responsibilities of a content designer. This can help you better understand the skills and knowledge needed for this role.

I've included a few examples of content design and UX writing job requirements and responsibilities from LinkedIn to help you get started.

UX Content Designer

Responsibilities:

- Create engaging and effective online content (microcopy, labels, page body copy, error messages, tooltips, help articles, emails, documents, and announcements).

- Create content for portal products, software applications, and user communications. Proofread the content for grammar, style, and tone of voice.

- Work with UX and UI designers to create delightful and effortless UX experiences through content design principles and well-balanced layouts with a finely tuned copy.

- Optimize the performance of UX writing via user testing and data validation.

- Combine data-driven and user-centric methodologies for better results.

- Collaborate with product owners, developers, and designers to translate business goals into unique brand and product experiences.

- Participate in all stages of the project lifecycle, such as requirements gathering, user analysis, testing, implementation, and result analysis.

Skills and competencies:

- 4+ years of UX content experience.

- An excellent team player with past experience working with agile teams.

- Knowledge of Microsoft Office applications such as Word, Excel, and Outlook.

- Knowledge of information architecture, interactive design principles, web usability, SEO, taxonomy, and metadata is desirable.

- Desirable: experience with Miro, Figma, or other similar tools.

- Desirable: experience with activation workflows or in-app messaging.

- Advanced English level.

Senior Content Designer

Responsibilities:

- Equal balance of copywriting and content design
- B2C
- Work on mobile apps in the health tech space
- Work on multiple products in the membership/ conversion space
- Multiple products - 1 is focused on converting people to become members, 1 is focused on upselling memberships within the app, 1 is focused on onboarding customers to product
- Focus on converting people to move from visiting the website to downloading the mobile app
- Meetings as needed - highly collaborative
- Collaboration with designers
- Slack for communication
- No touch, low touch, and high touch support for designers
- Check copy grammar/typos, design critiques, and product design review

Skills and competencies:

- 2-5+ years of Content Design, UX Writing, and Content Strategy experience
- Balance of copywriting and content design - selling people on things and teaching them how to use the product
- Copywriting chops in the product space
- Engagement, growth application experience (membership growth)
- B2C experience
- Writing for mobile (mobile web or mobile app)
- Experience with content writing for customer engagement, retention, etc., in the mobile space
- Experience partnering with product designers, PMs, and marketing
- Complex, innovative, cross-functional matrix environment
- Figma
- Mobile, Product tech industry experience (finance and e-commerce would be a good fit for this role)
- Portfolio

Content Design Lead

Responsibilities:

- Own product copy and content strategy for the entire product area, including client and agent experiences.

- Demonstrate the impact of your work proactively and often. Use data and customer insights to guide your work and advocate for it.

- Partner with Product Marketing, UX Research, Product Management, and other cross-functional colleagues to develop a consistent voice, tone, and taxonomy for product features.

- Help build and implement processes, resources, and standards for the Content Design team.

- Be an active and available peer mentor for other writers and contribute to our positive and collaborative team culture.

- Hire other writers and expand the Content Design function to better support product delivery.

Skills and competencies:

- An outstanding portfolio of your work with a proven track record of explaining complex things in a simple and digestible way. Like real people talking to each other.

- Experience in product writing, content design, and/or copywriting, with a demonstrated record of writing successful UX/UI copy with measurable impact.

- Proficiency in Figma, Sketch, or equivalent design tools to collaborate with designers alongside their work.

- Experience creating style guides, content standards, or related artifacts to help others write successfully.

- Ability to track the impact of your work across multiple teams and to proactively manage issues and complexity.

- Experience advocating for content and design and driving projects forward.

- Experience building teams over time through hiring, growing, and keeping high-performing employees is a huge bonus.

Manager, UX Writing and Content Design

Responsibilities:

- Manages a team of writers across various levels of experience and expertise, including their performance and progression and owns workability cases

- Ensures the development of individuals within the organization. Coaches and mentors individual writers to improve craft, deliverables, communication and career advancement.

- Evaluates and elevates individuals' process, strategy and craft through critique, review or other measurable steps.

- Identifies headcount needs for writers aligned to track or business goals. Works with HR and UX Writing and Content Design leadership to recruit and interview candidates.

- Works with individuals and groups to define clear and measurable day-to-day working goals aligned with business and stakeholder needs

- Helps reports prioritize work on product and community-focused initiatives and projects. Guides the definition of team distribution to capitalize on their reports' strengths and maintain focus.

- Demonstrates experience managing complex and high-level stakeholders, processes, business priorities and projects, and the ability to influence and guide individuals. Manages up and down effectively.

- Networks across multiple teams, tracks and disciplines to achieve objectives, proactively builds productive relationships across teams

Skills and competencies:

- Acts as a subject matter expert on UX writing, copy and translations systems and tooling, as well as their product area or business topic. Understands the right balance between quality and velocity.

- Advances reports' understanding and application of user-centered strategy and techniques to enable and advance quality UX writing and messaging outcomes. Leads by example through practical hands-on work when/if necessary.

- Encourages and enables their direct reports in facilitating workshops, sprints, critiques, reviews, or other collaborative processes across teams or tracks to engage direct reports, peers, and key stakeholders to provide continual direction for UX writing and content strategy

- Develops and drives improvement or implementation plans to relevant UX writing and translation systems and guidelines. Works with UX design and writing leadership, as well as others to ensure product, craft, quality, and accessibility standards and requirements are applied across their reports' tracks, teams and products.

- Demonstrates awareness of current and upcoming trends in market, technology and UX writing. Shares this knowledge widely and encourages others to learn.

Source: Linkedin job advertisements

11. YOUR FIRST STEPS TOWARDS A CAREER IN CONTENT DESIGN

If you're ready to explore a career in content design, here is an approach to consider:

Evaluate your strengths and interests:

Content design requires various skills, including writing, problem-solving, collaboration, adaptability and multitasking. Consider your strengths and interests in these areas and how they align with the requirements of a content design role. Do you enjoy creating engaging content to solve a user and business problem? Are you interested in user experience and design thinking? If so, content design may be a good fit for you.

Pursue education or training to build your skills:

This can help you build the skills and knowledge needed for a career in content design and make you more competitive in the job market. Look for online courses, certificate programs, or degree programs in content design, user experience design, or related fields.

Gain experience and build your portfolio:

Building a portfolio will help you gain hands-on experience and demonstrate skills to potential employers. After pursuing an education in content design, you can apply your knowledge by taking on freelance or volunteer projects to create content and designs for websites, social media, or other digital platforms.

Seek mentorship and networking opportunities:

Networking with other professionals in the content design field can be a great way to learn more about the industry and gain insights into the day-to-day responsibilities of a content designer. Seek mentorship opportunities or attend industry events and conferences to connect with other professionals and learn more about the field.

12. GET STARTED WITH AN INTRODUCTORY CONTENT DESIGN COURSE

One of the best ways to prepare for a career in a new field is to study, learn and apply what you've learned. And there are resources you can explore, from books to courses and workshops. Here are recommendations:

1. **The UK government offers a free 4-week 'Introduction to Content Design' course** on Future Learn. Check out the course website to sign up.

2. **The UX Content Collective offers a certified** 'Fundamentals of UX Writing' online course. The course costs $1600.

3. **The UX Writing Hub offers a** free online course.

RESOURCES

Rahel Anne Bailie & Noz Urbina. (2012). *Content Strategy: Connecting the Dots Between Business, Brand, and Benefits.* XML Press.

Sarah Richards. (2017). *Content Design.* Content Design London.

About STC. https://www.stc.org/about-stc/

Yuval Keshtcher. (2022). *UX Writing Salaries in 2022: Survey Report.* https://uxwritinghub.com/ux-writing-salary-survey

ABOUT THE AUTHOR

Azza Elarabi is a highly skilled content strategist and writer with over 12 years of experience in the field. Her expertise spans various areas, including editorial, ecommerce, brand positioning, UX writing, and content design.

Azza has worked with multinational organizations to help them effectively communicate with their audiences and customers. Her ability to create compelling content that engages readers and drives results has earned her a reputation as a trusted advisor in the industry.

Azza's educational background includes a master's degree in content strategy from FH Joanneum University in Austria, which has equipped her with the knowledge and skills to create effective content strategies aligned with business objectives.

Azza enjoys reading, writing, and traveling to new places in her free time. She is passionate about staying current with the latest trends and innovations in content strategy and is committed to helping organizations and practitioners achieve their goals through impactful content.

Contact Azza on Linkedin.

www.ingramcontent.com/pod-product-compliance
Lightning Source LLC
Chambersburg PA
CBHW040400220526
45473CB00025B/2755